T0023803

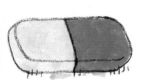

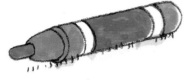

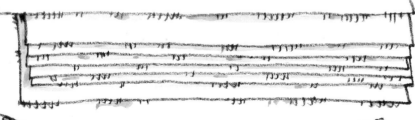

To: _____

From: _____

In memory of Mr. Robert Beck,
St. Luke's School for Boys,
New Canaan, Connecticut

—Huck Scarry

Visit us on the Web! rhcbooks.com
richardscarry.com

Educators and librarians, for a variety of teaching tools,
visit us at RHTeachersLibrarians.com

Editor: Frank Berrios | Designer: Marianna Smirnova
Copy Editor: Bess Schelper Sampson
Managing Editor: Julie Gayle
Production Manager: Luke McCord

ISBN 978-0-593-70629-9 (hardcover)

MANUFACTURED IN CHINA
10 9 8 7 6 5 4 3 2 1
First Edition

Richard Scarry's
BEST TEACHER
EVER!

Random House 🏠 New York

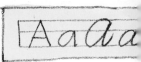

You help me learn my **ABC**s.

You guide me

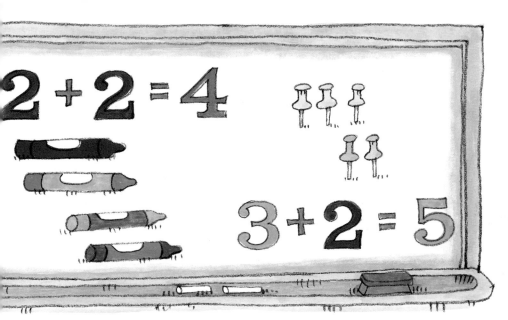

$$2 + 2 = 4$$

$$3 + 2 = 5$$

through the **123**s.

You help me keep

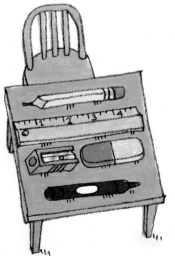

things NICE and NEAT . . .

... and always make learning such a **TREAT**!

You find my talents

and help them **GROW**.

You teach me
things I didn't
KNOW!

Teachers make learning so much **FUN**!

We LAUGH

and **LEARN**

till the day is done!

There really is no
CONTEST.....

Being a teacher

must be the **BEST**!

You are **PATIENT,**

KiND,

and CLEVER.

To **ME**, you are the
BEST
TEACHER
EVER!

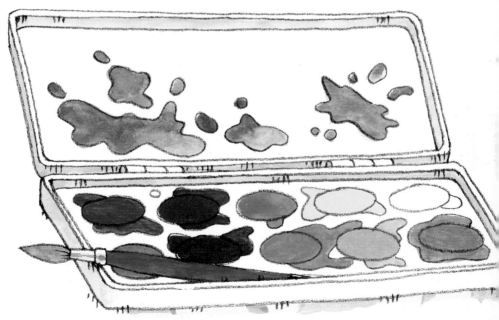